Knights
and
Dragons

Room 1

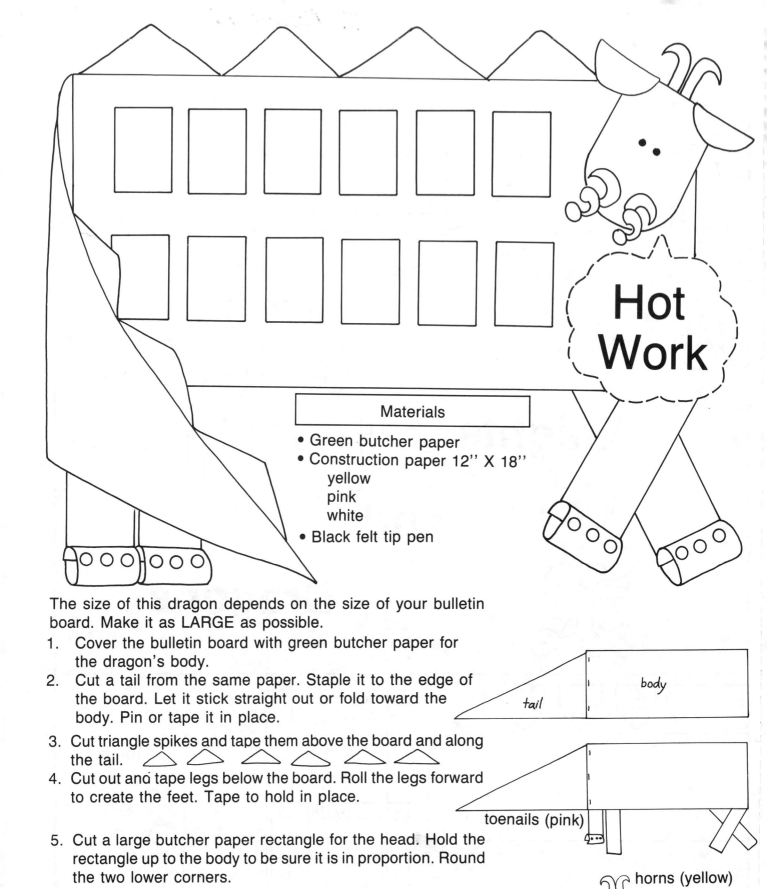

Hot Work

Materials

- Green butcher paper
- Construction paper 12" X 18"
  - yellow
  - pink
  - white
- Black felt tip pen

The size of this dragon depends on the size of your bulletin board. Make it as LARGE as possible.

1. Cover the bulletin board with green butcher paper for the dragon's body.
2. Cut a tail from the same paper. Staple it to the edge of the board. Let it stick straight out or fold toward the body. Pin or tape it in place.
3. Cut triangle spikes and tape them above the board and along the tail.
4. Cut out and tape legs below the board. Roll the legs forward to create the feet. Tape to hold in place.
5. Cut a large butcher paper rectangle for the head. Hold the rectangle up to the body to be sure it is in proportion. Round the two lower corners.
6. Cut a speech bubble from white construction paper. Letter the caption with black felt pen.

body

tail

toenails (pink)

horns (yellow)
ears (green)
eyes (black pen)
nostrils (pink)

2   Room Themes

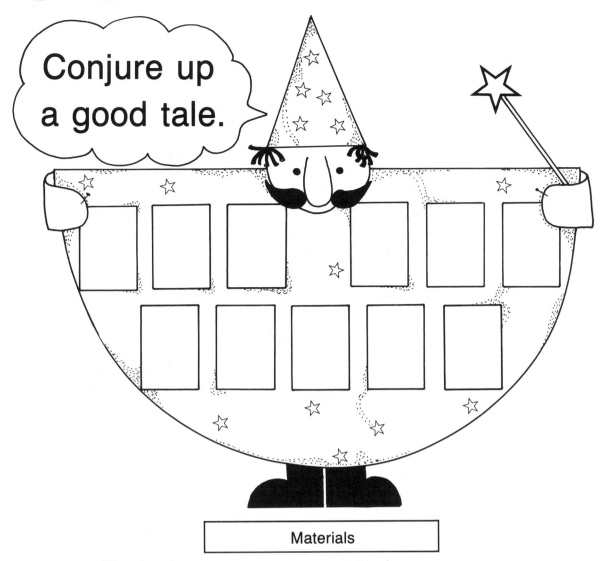

Conjure up a good tale.

Materials

- Blue butcher paper
- Construction paper 12'' X 18''
  - white
  - black
- Black yarn
- 1 straw
- Silver and gold star stickers
- Black felt pen

If you can, make this wizard large enough to actually put his feet on the floor.

1. Roll out the blue butcher paper on the floor. Make the piece long enough to fill your bulletin board area. Fold it in half and round off the corner. Pin it to the bulletin board.
2. Cut a large white construction paper circle for the head. Lay it on the body to be sure it is in proportion. Add eyes and a nose with felt pen. Cut the moustache from black construction paper. Glue it to the face.
3. Cut a tall triangular hat that fits on the head. Glue it in place. Slip pieces of black yarn under each side of the hat for hair. Tape the head to the body.
4. Cut hands from white construction paper. Pin them behind the blue paper body. Bend the hands around to the front and pin them in place. Tape the straw with a star on the end in one of the wizard's hands.
5. Cut out two black shoes. Tape them below the body.
6. Scatter star stickers around the body and hat.
7. Cut a speech bubble from large white construction paper. Add the caption with black felt pen.

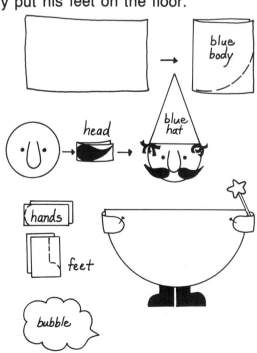

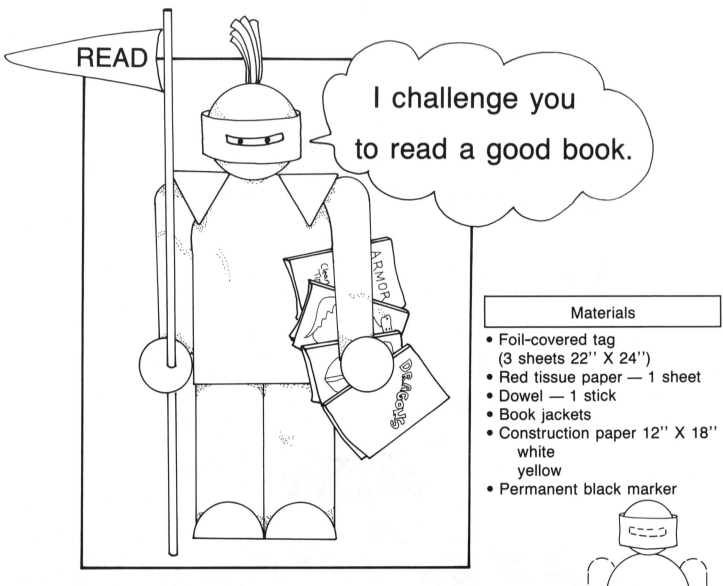

READ

I challenge you to read a good book.

Materials

- Foil-covered tag (3 sheets 22'' X 24'')
- Red tissue paper — 1 sheet
- Dowel — 1 stick
- Book jackets
- Construction paper 12'' X 18''
  white
  yellow
- Permanent black marker

1. Cut the knight's armor from foil-covered tag. (You may cover regular tag with aluminum foil for the same effect.) Pin the parts together on the bulletin board. Add details with the black marker. Cut a strip out of the face mask with an exacto knife. Roll the ends behind the head and tape in place.

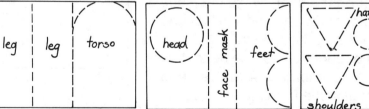

leg	leg	torso
head	face mask	feet
hands	shoulders	arm arm

2. Accordion-fold the red tissue paper. Pin it behind the helmet. Spread it apart to form the plume.

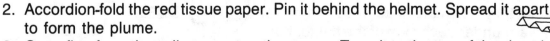

3. Cut a flag from the yellow construction paper. Tape it to the top of the dowel. Cut a slice in one of the knight's hands. Slip the dowel into the center of the cut. Pin or tape the dowel in place. Write READ on the flag with the black marker.

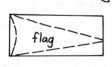

flag

4. Cut a speech bubble from the white construction paper. Letter caption with black felt pen.
5. Tuck book jackets under the arm and in the hand of the knight.
6. Place a display table in front of the bulletin board. Set out a selection of books about knights and the medieval times.

bubble

This damsel is in distress.
Can you tell her the date?

Materials

- 1 calendar face
- Yellow butcher paper
- Reproduce the pattern on page 6
- 1 small scarf
- Felt pens

S	M	T	W	TH	F	S

1. Reproduce, color, and cut out the princess pattern on page 6.
2. Roll out the yellow butcher paper on the floor. Cut a long strip for the turret. Notch the top edge. Pin it to the bulletin board.

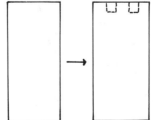

3. Paste the picture of the princess towards the top part of the turret. Pin the calendar face over the turret.
4. Attach a small scarf to the top of the princess' hat.

Reproduce on card stock, color with felt pens, cut on the dotted line, and use with the calendar bulletin board on page 5.

Attach a small scarf here.

Room Themes

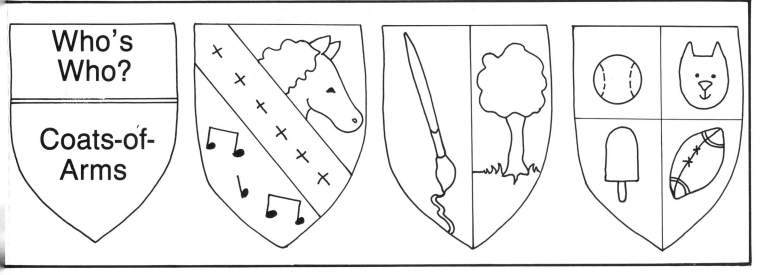

Who's
Who?

Coats-of-
Arms

Research and discuss with your students the significance of the coats-of-arms that covered the shields of the medieval knights. The knights carried identifying marks on their shields because their faces were often covered by armor. The shields provided quick identification of friend and foe. The shield designs were passed down through families, but each knight's coat-of-arms was personalized in some way to make it unique.

The Knights by Michael Gibson; Arco Publishing, Inc., 1984 is a good book on the subject of shields and coats-of-arms to share with your students.

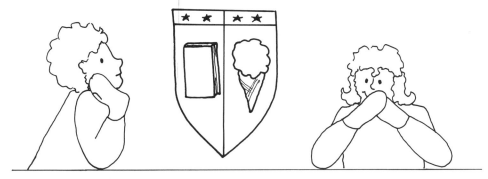

Reproduce the shield pattern on page 8. Let your students create their own shield designs. The design could depict some aspect of their names or a favorite pet, hobby, or sport they enjoy. Display the finished shields above the chalkboard. Let the class try to figure out to whom each shield belongs by reading the clues in the design.

You may also cut writing paper to fit behind the shield designs so that students can write an explanation of their design. Staple or pin the writing paper and shield together at the top.

Coat-of-Arms

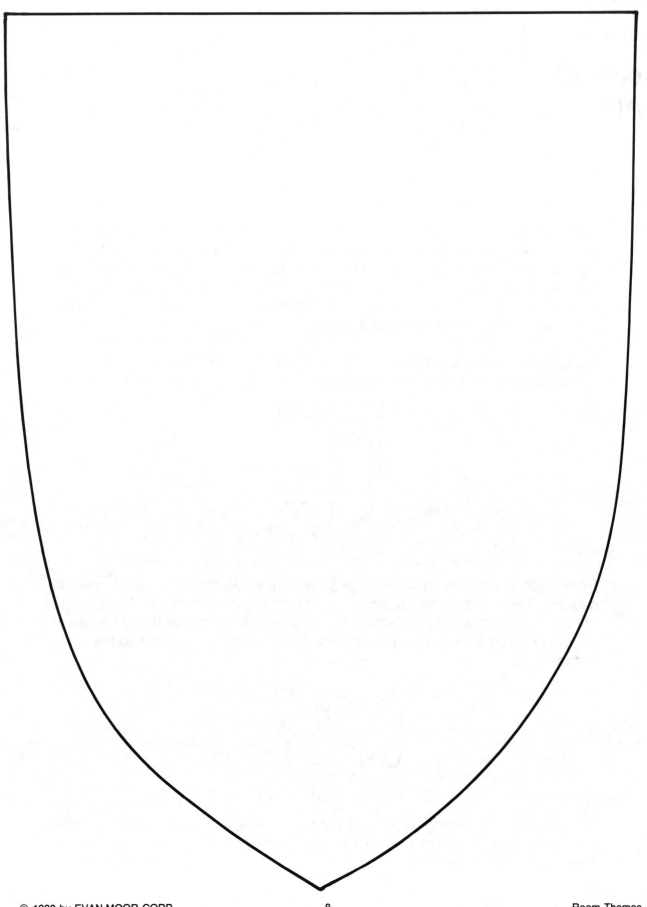

      8   Room Themes

Castle Display Board

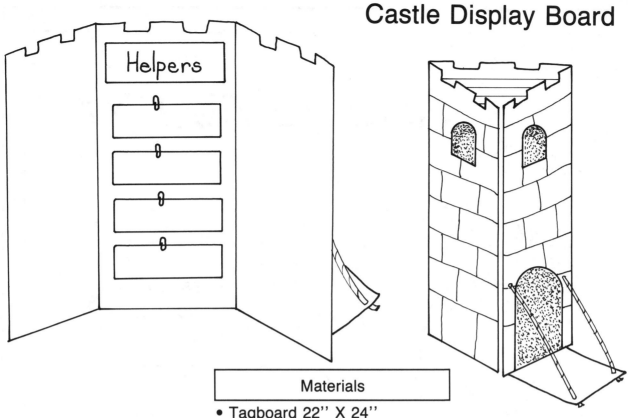

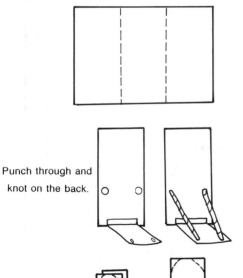

Punch through and knot on the back.

Materials

- Tagboard 22" X 24" (any color)
- Construction paper (assorted colors)
- Yarn

1. Fold the tagboard into thirds. It will fold easily if you first score along the line with an exacto knife and a straight edge. Reinforce this fold line with transparent tape.

2. Cut out small boxes along the top edge.

3. Cut a rectangular piece of tagboard for a drawbridge. Tape it to the front flap of the castle along the lower edge. Attach two strips of yarn to the free end of the drawbridge. Attach the other ends of the yarn to the castle wall.

4. Cut a large arch for the gate and small arched windows from a contrasting color of construction paper. Glue them to the castle. Add grid lines that resemble blocks with a black felt pen.

How can you use this castle?

- List your helpers each week on sentence strips. Tape the strips to the inside of the castle.
- Use the castle as a creative writing center by listing story starters or vocabulary inside the castle.
- Make this into a castle book by stapling finished stories inside the castle.

You can make this an individual award by changing the type on the banner.

Hear Ye Hear Ye

These students have shown themselves to be outstanding.

Reading Robot

Good Work Machine

Help u

Robots

January

S M T W Th F S

Room 1

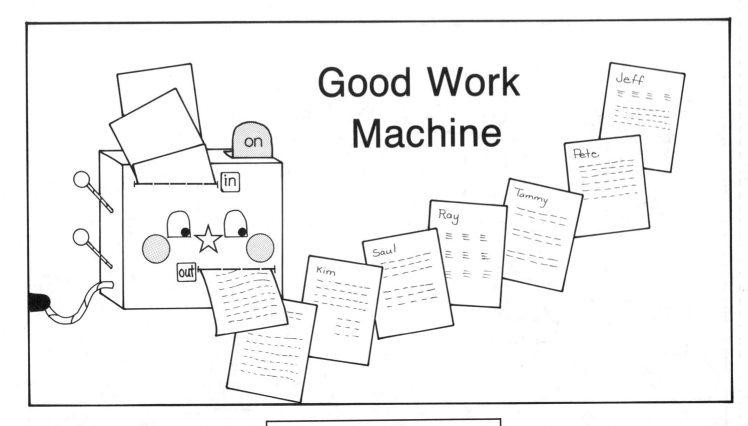

Good Work Machine

- Large box top
- 2 straws
- Blue butcher paper or contact paper (box)
- Yellow butcher paper (background)

- Construction paper scraps
  red
  black
  white
- Black yarn
- Samples of children's work

Background

Cover the bulletin board with yellow butcher paper.

Machine

1. Cover the box top with blue paper.

2. Cut features from construction paper. Add details with black pen. Glue them to the box.

3. Make slits with scissors. Write in and out with black pen.

4. Make the levers from straws and construction paper. Punch holes in the box and stick in the ends of the straws. Secure them by dropping a little glue in each hole.

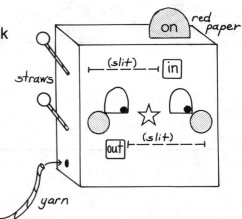

Caption

Cut letters from red construction paper.

Work Samples

Pin blank work pages or writing paper in the "in" slot. Randomly pin the children's finished work coming out of the "out" slot and scattered across the board.

Robot Dis...

1. Fold the tagboard into thirds.

Materials

- 1/2 sheet of tagboard (11" X 24")
- 3 copies of the Robot Buddy on page 21
- Felt pens

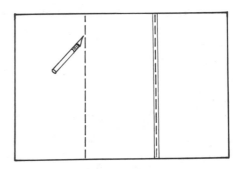

Score with an exacto knife along fold lines. Reinforce with transparent tape.

2. Color the three Robot Buddies. Cut on the dotted lines. Open the flaps on each robot's chest.

3. Paste one robot in each section of the tagboard. Hide surprises inside each flap.

How to use:

- Use one robot as a stu... ...ighlight center. Tape a picture of the student inside the flaps.

Help us sort out our tools!

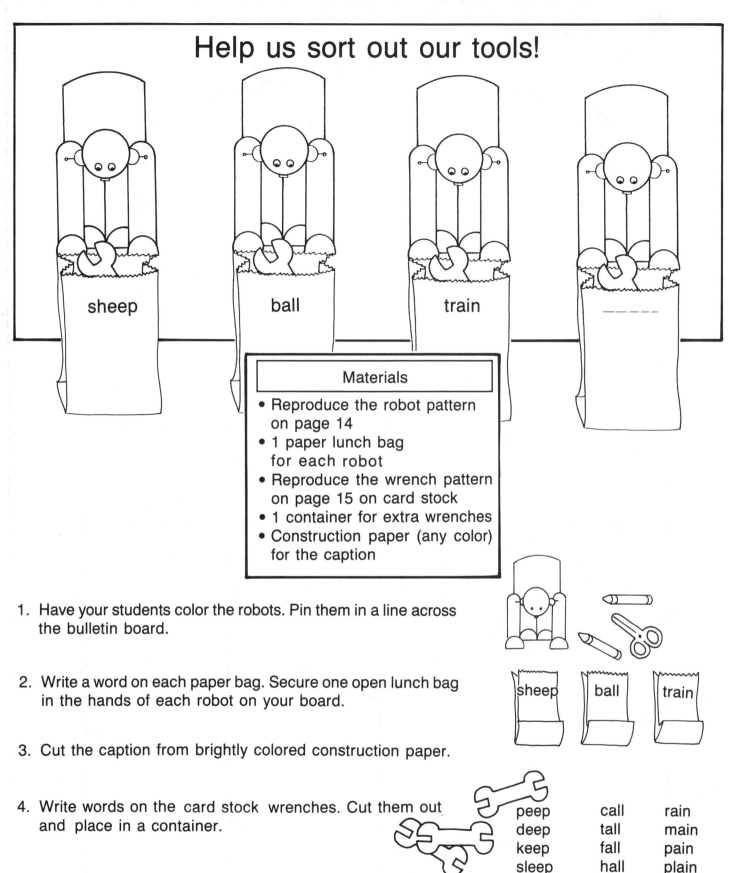

sheep   ball   train   _____

Materials

- Reproduce the robot pattern on page 14
- 1 paper lunch bag for each robot
- Reproduce the wrench pattern on page 15 on card stock
- 1 container for extra wrenches
- Construction paper (any color) for the caption

1. Have your students color the robots. Pin them in a line across the bulletin board.

2. Write a word on each paper bag. Secure one open lunch bag in the hands of each robot on your board.

3. Cut the caption from brightly colored construction paper.

4. Write words on the card stock wrenches. Cut them out and place in a container.

peep	call	rain
deep	tall	main
keep	fall	pain
sleep	hall	plain

How to use:

This board can be used to reinforce a variety of reading/language skills. The sample board shows word families. Children are to select a wrench from the container, read the word, and place it in the correct paper bag. Other uses would be contractions, word meanings, categories, etc.

13

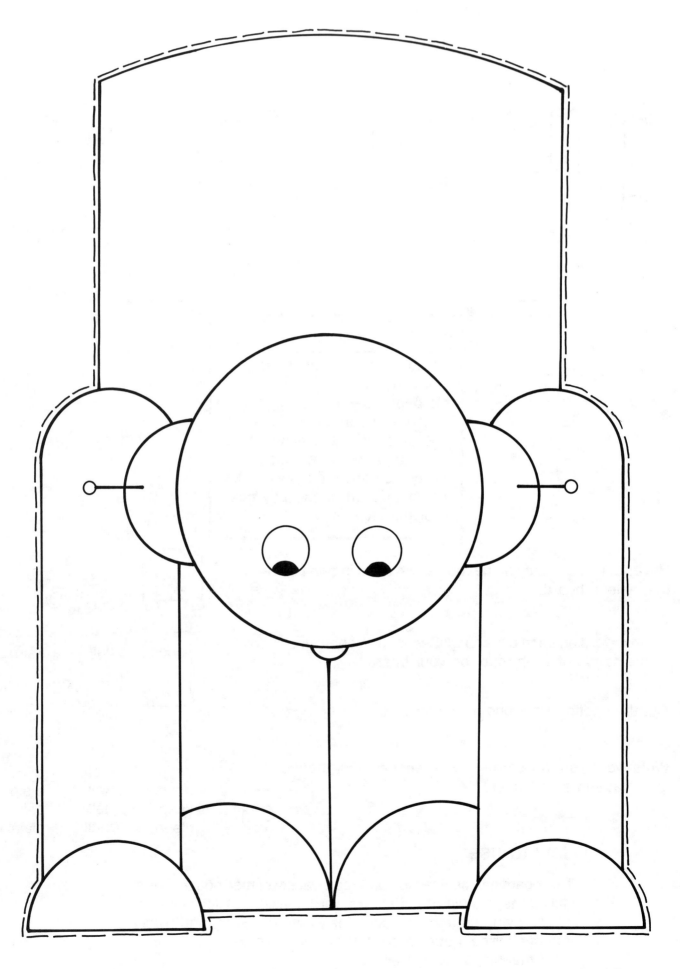

Reproduce these wrenches on tagboard. Use with page 13.

A Reading Robot

1. Cover the paper towel rolls, tissue paper rolls, and paper plate with aluminum foil.

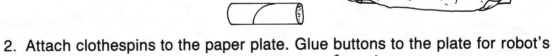

2. Attach clothespins to the paper plate. Glue buttons to the plate for robot's eyes. Add a smile with a black felt pen.

3. Pin the robot's head to the bulletin board. Pin a muffin cup on each side of the head. Staple book jackets overlapping each other.

4. Pin the arm and leg rolls in place. Slip garden gloves on the ends of the rolls.

5. Cut the caption from red letters and staple above the robot.

S	M	T	W	TH	F	S

1. Cover the paper towel rolls, tissue paper rolls, and paper plate with aluminum foil.

2. Attach the clothespins to the paper plate. Glue buttons to the plate for robot's eyes. Add a smile with a black felt pen.

3. Pin the robot's head to the bulletin board. Pin a muffin cup on each side of the head. Staple the calendar face below it. Pin the arms and legs into place.

4. Letter the name of the month on the red construction paper. Pin the paper in the robot's hands.

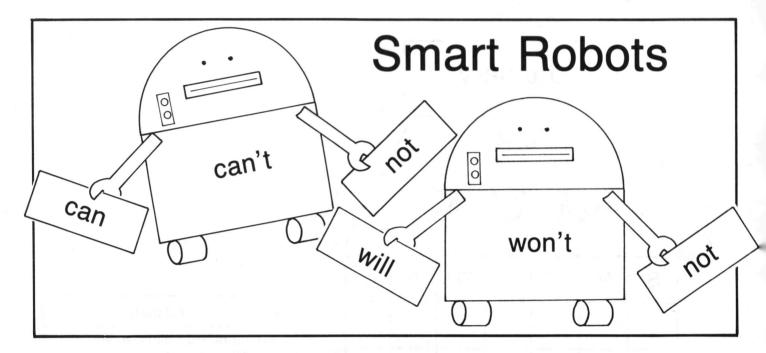

Smart Robots

Use this little robot to reinforce any language or math skills you may be working on with your class. (Make enough to go across the top of your chalkboard.)

Reproduce the robot pattern on page 19. Let children help make the robots by coloring them and adding their arms.

Make cards appropriate to the skill you are practicing to place on the front of the robot and in its hands.

Practice contraction forms.

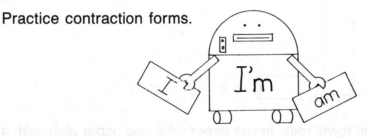

Practice math facts.

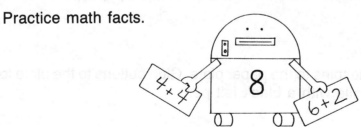

Create a line of robots with the ordinal (or Roman Numeral) numbers on them.

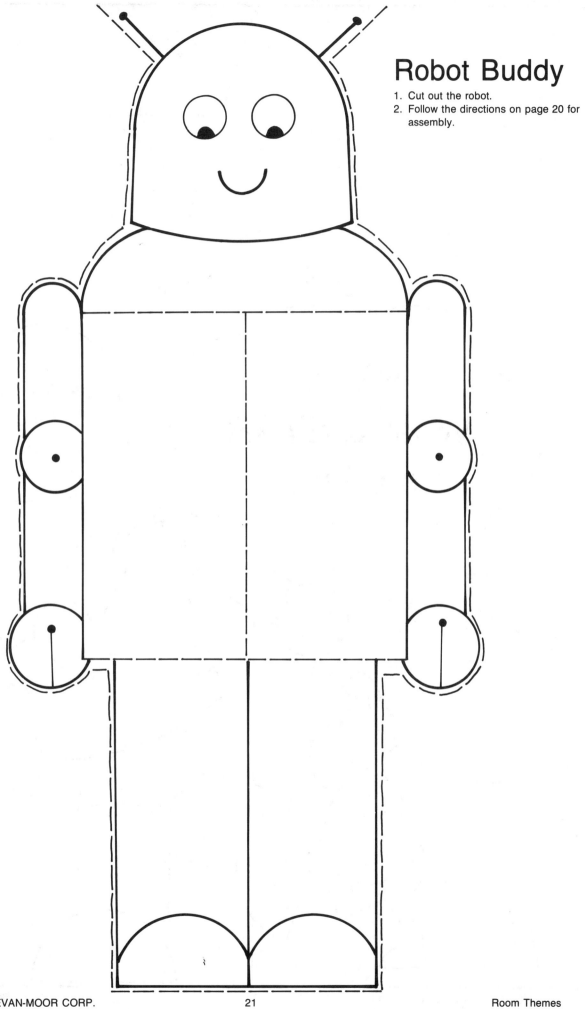

Robot Buddy

1. Cut out the robot.
2. Follow the directions on page 20 for assembly.

Room Themes

Room Themes

Reach for a good book.

Star Work

Under the Sea

Room 1

Room Themes

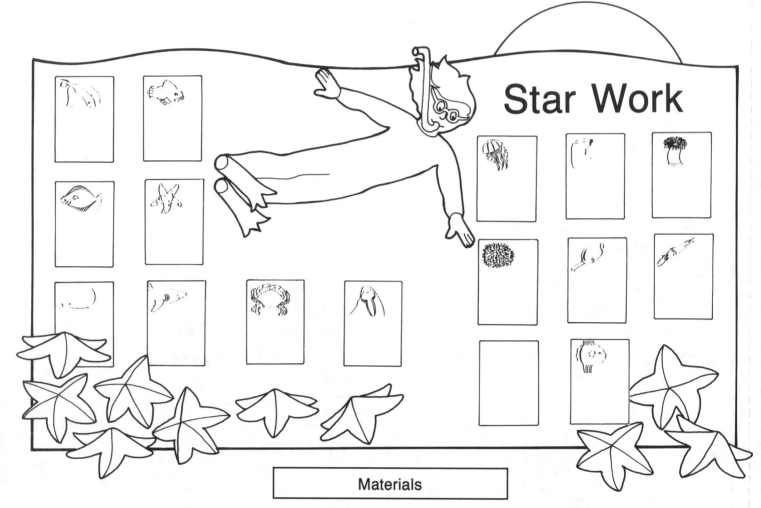

Star Work

Materials

- Blue and yellow butcher paper
- Scuba Diver — pattern page 25
- Starfish — directions page 26
- Student papers — use the picture cards on page 27 to stimulate creative writing about undersea creatures.

1. Cover the bulletin board with blue butcher paper. Cut the top edge in a wavy line.

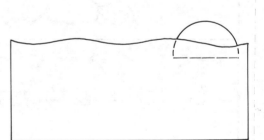

2. Cut one half of a large yellow sun from butcher paper. Slip it behind the blue butcher paper.

3. Reproduce the scuba diver. Use as many as your bulletin board will hold. (Let your students color them for you.)

4. Pin up the starfish that your students have made following the directions on page 26.

5. Display students' work papers.

NOTE — Stretch a large sheet of clear plastic over the entire bulletin board to give the appearance of being under water. You can purchase it at your local yardage store.

Room Themes

This pattern can be enlarged if you have a BIG bulletin board to fill.

Room Themes

How to make paper plate starfish:

1. Draw a starfish on the back of a paper plate. (You may want to make a template for younger children to trace.)

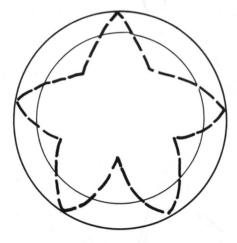

2. Cut out the starfish. Color the top and bottom.

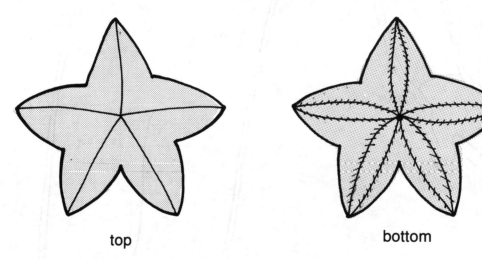

top   bottom

3. Pinch each arm for a 3-D look.

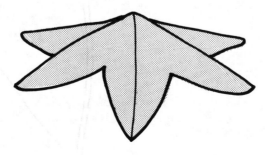

26

Reproduce this page. Cut the cards apart. Use them to stimulate creative writing. Give one card to each student to paste in the corner of a sheet of writing paper. The child then writes on that topic.

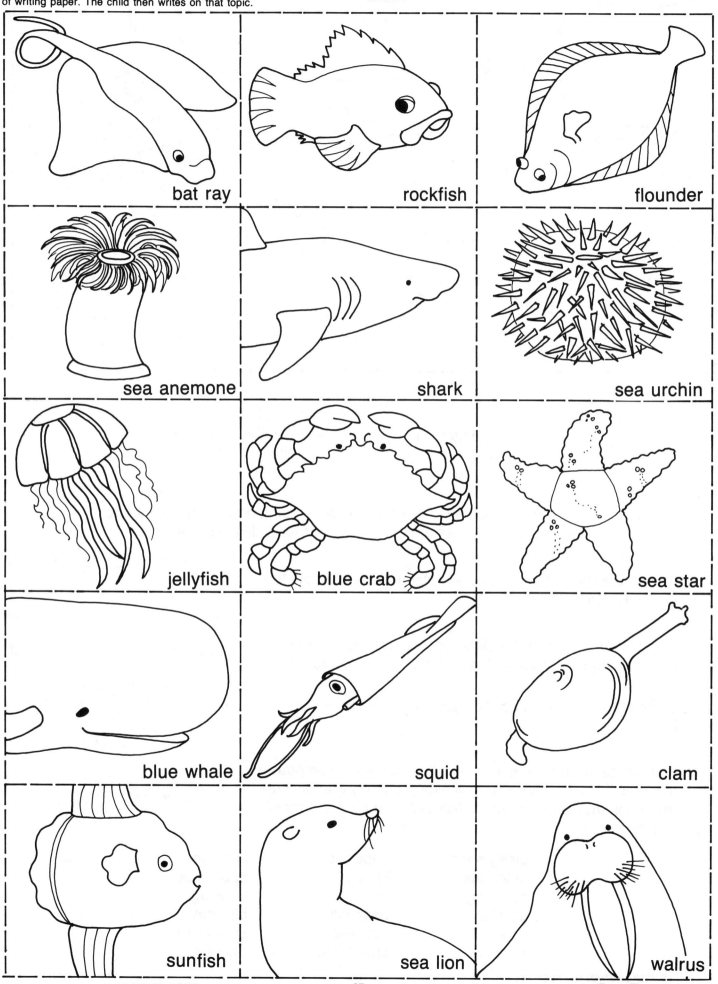

bat ray

rockfish

flounder

sea anemone

shark

sea urchin

jellyfish

blue crab

sea star

blue whale

squid

clam

sunfish

sea lion

walrus

Room Themes

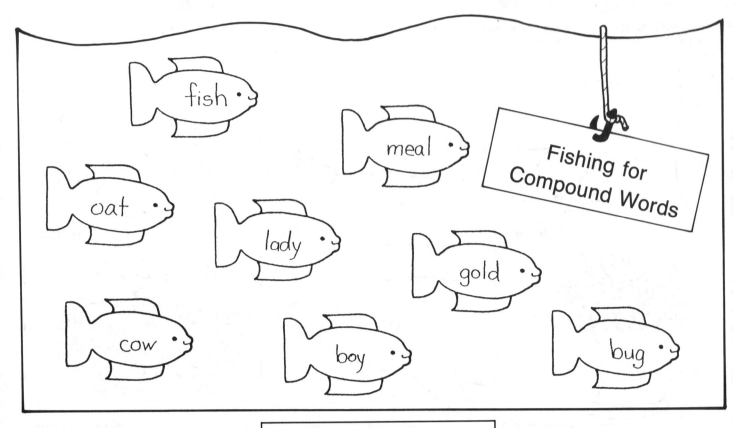

Fishing for Compound Words

Materials

- Fish pattern on page 29
- Blue butcher paper
- Black yarn

- Construction paper
  black
  white

This board is a helpful activity to do with a group needing practice in compound words. It can also be used as a free-time center for individual practice.

1. Cover the bulletin board with blue butcher paper. Cut the top in a wavy line.

2. Use a strip of yarn and a black construction paper hook to hold the sign that reads Fishing for Compound Words.

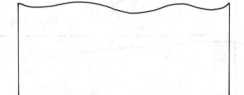

3. Write 1/2 a compound word on each fish. Pin the fish on the board.

4. Let students try to match up the correct "compound couples." How many can they make? (You may want to write the ones they find on the chalkboard so they don't repeat themselves.)

playground	cupcake	sunshine
broomstick	fireman	applesauce
butterfly	into	ladybug
goldfish	baseball	birthday
cowboy	oatmeal	snowflake
airplane	chopsticks	pancake

Room Themes

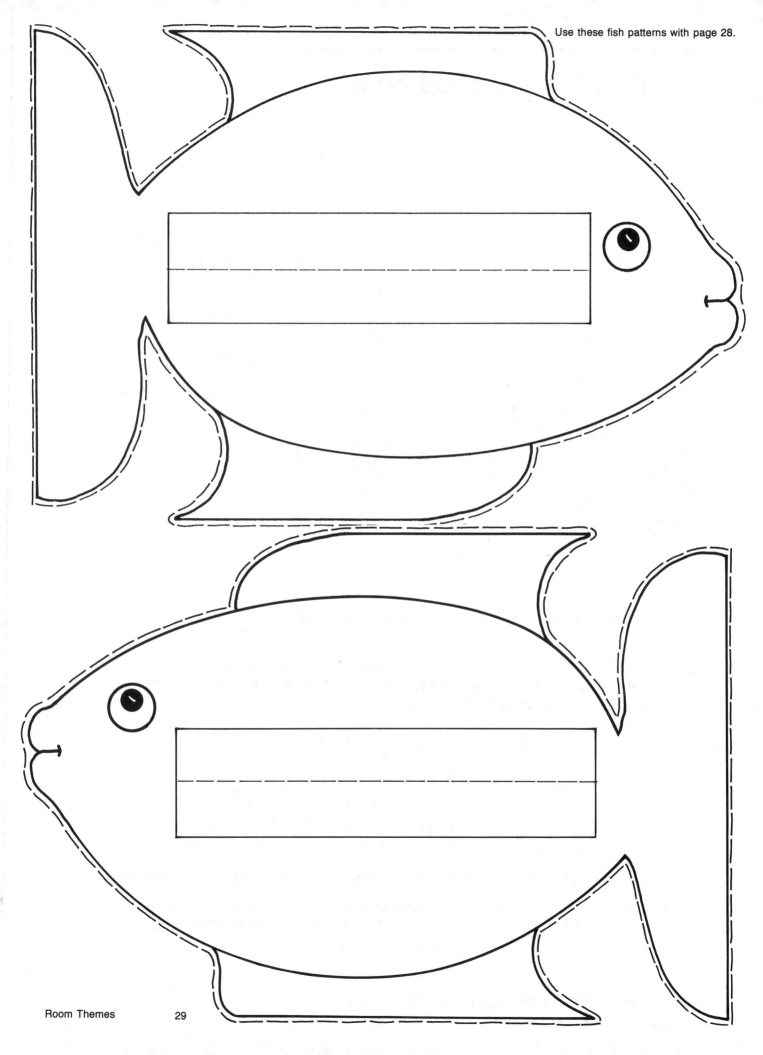

Reach for a good book!

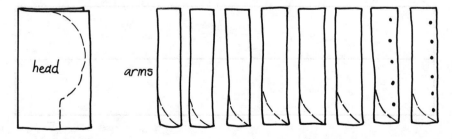

Materials

- Blue butcher paper
- Pink butcher paper
- Construction paper
    white
    black
- Red 3/4'' round stickers
- Felt pens
- Assorted book jackets

1. Cover the bulletin board with the blue butcher paper.

2. Cut pink butcher paper to make the octopus. Make it as large as possible. Cut the head on the fold. Cut eight tentacles. Add red sticker circles on the straight edge of each tentacle for suction cups.

Let the tentacles of this octopus reach beyond the limits of your bulletin board.

3. Cut eyes from the white and black construction paper. Paste them to the octopus. Add a smile with a felt tip pen. Pin a book jacket in each tentacle.

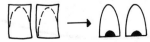

4. Cut the letters for the caption from black paper.

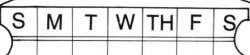

Mermaids prefer ____.
(month)

S	M	T	W	TH	F	S

Materials

• Butcher paper
    pink (skin)
    green (tail)
• Yellow construction paper
• Calendar face
• Felt pens
• Glue

1. Cut the pieces for the mermaid's upper body. Cut a pink circle for the mermaid's head. Add details with felt tip pen. Lay the calendar on a strip of pink butcher paper. Cut a strip for the arms making it long enough to wrap around the calendar face.

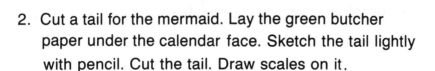

2. Cut a tail for the mermaid. Lay the green butcher paper under the calendar face. Sketch the tail lightly with pencil. Cut the tail. Draw scales on it.

3. The mermaid's hair is cut from yellow construction paper. Cut strips and curl them around a pencil. Cut some shorter strips for bangs. Glue the hair to the head piece.

4. Pin the mermaid to the board. Pin some of the strips of paper to the board, twisting some to give a 3-D effect.

Guess Who I Am

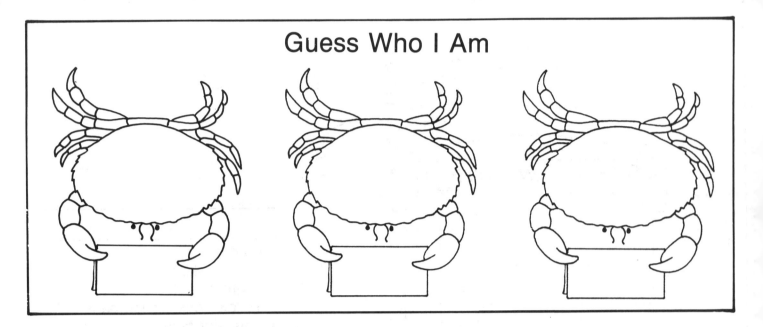

Materials

- Reproduce the crab pattern on page 33.
- Construction paper
- Felt pens

This is a useful bulletin board idea for that long, narrow space above your chalkboard.

1. Make a chart listing riddles about underwater life.
2. Reproduce the crab pattern on page 33. Invite students to color and cut out the crabs. Display the crabs on the bulletin board.
3. Pin a piece of folded construction paper in the claws of each crab. Put a number on the outside of each of these cards that corresponds to the numbers of the riddles on the chart. Write the answer to the riddles inside the cards.
4. Each day read a riddle with your class and verify the answers by peeking inside the card.

You may use the same procedure to practice solving word problems in math, matching words with their meaning, or answering questions from social studies or science studies.

Suggested riddles:

1. I am shy. I hide in rocks. I can change color. My 8 tentacles help me move and catch my food. (octopus)
2. I am small. I have no shell of my own. I make my home in the empty shells of other sea creatures. (hermit crab)
3. I have many arms. I move along the bottom of the sea. I use my arms to hold onto rocks and my food. (starfish)
4. I have gills to help me breathe under the water. I have fins to help me swim along. (fish)
5. I am the largest animal in the sea. I look somewhat like a fish, but I am a mammal. (whale)
6. I have a flat shell. Sometimes when I am opened up, a pearl is found inside of me. (oyster)

Use this crab pattern with page 32.

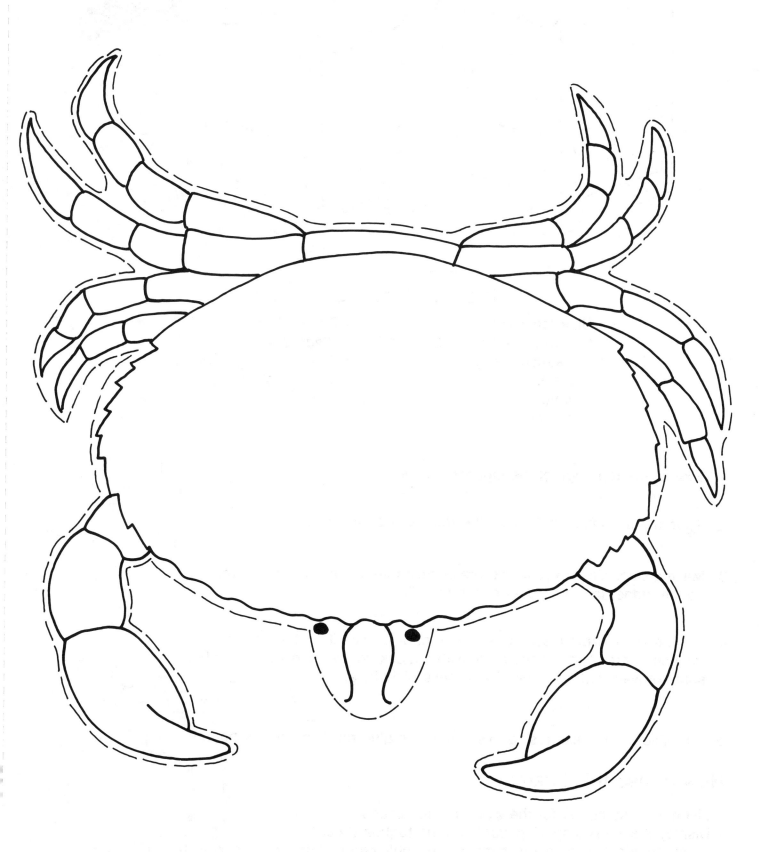

Room Themes

Underwater Display Board

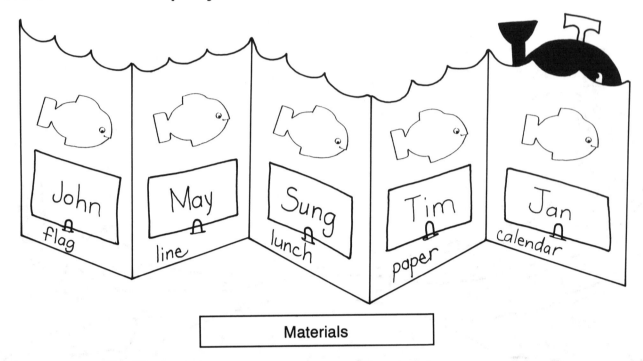

Materials

- Blue tagboard
  (Cut each section 8 1/2" X 11")
- Construction paper
  - black
  - white
  - orange
- Paper clips
- Clear tape
- Tagboard strips cut into
  4" X 7 1/2" cards

1. Scallop the top edge of the tagboard sections.

2. Tape the sections together on the front and on the back.

3. Make a small slit with your scissors in the center of each board 2" from the bottom edge. Insert a paper clip in the slit.

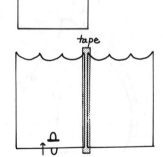

4. Cut the whale from black construction paper. Tape it on the back side of the first board. Add a white circle with a black dot for an eye. Cut a white spray of water coming from the whale's blow hole.

5. Cut little orange fish (using this pattern) to glue randomly to the boards.

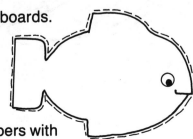

How to use this board:

- List one class helper for the week in each section.
- Display the week's spelling words on the tagboard cards.
- Display student work papers that deserve highlighting. Attach the papers with clothespins to the top of each section.

       Room Themes

What a Treasure!

name

Room Themes

Under the Big Top

Tame thos

READ

The Circus

Room 1

Room Themes

Under the Big Top

Materials	

• Butcher paper
  yellow
  blue
  orange
• 1 yardstick
	• Reproduce the clown patterns
	  on pages 38 & 39
	• Writing paper
	• Black tempera paint and
	  a 1'' brush

This circus tent can fill one whole wall of your classroom. Don't be confined by a small rectangular bulletin board!

Tent

1. Roll out blue butcher paper in front of your bulletin board area. Decide on the length and width you will need for the tent. Fold the piece in half and cut the open end at a slant. Tape or staple the paper in place on your board.
2. Roll out the yellow butcher paper for the top of the tent. Cut it off at the same length as the blue tent. Fold the strip in half. Cut the pointed top and scalloped bottom. Staple or tape the top of the tent in place.
3. Roll out a strip of orange butcher paper for the flag. Cut a pointed flag. Letter the caption on the tent with a 1'' brush and black tempera paint. Tape the end of the flag to the yardstick. Tape the flag and stick to the top of the tent.

Clowns

Reproduce the clown's face on page 38 and the clown's legs on page 39. Have your students write stories about the circus on regular writing paper. Paste the clown face to the top of the story and the feet to the bottom of the story. The feet can be attached in several different ways.

Let the clowns tumble across the bulletin board. You can add animals or other circus characters to the big top scene.

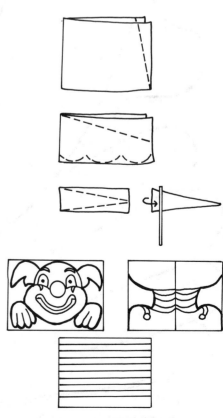

Reproduce this pattern and the one on the following page for the Under the Big Top bulletin board.

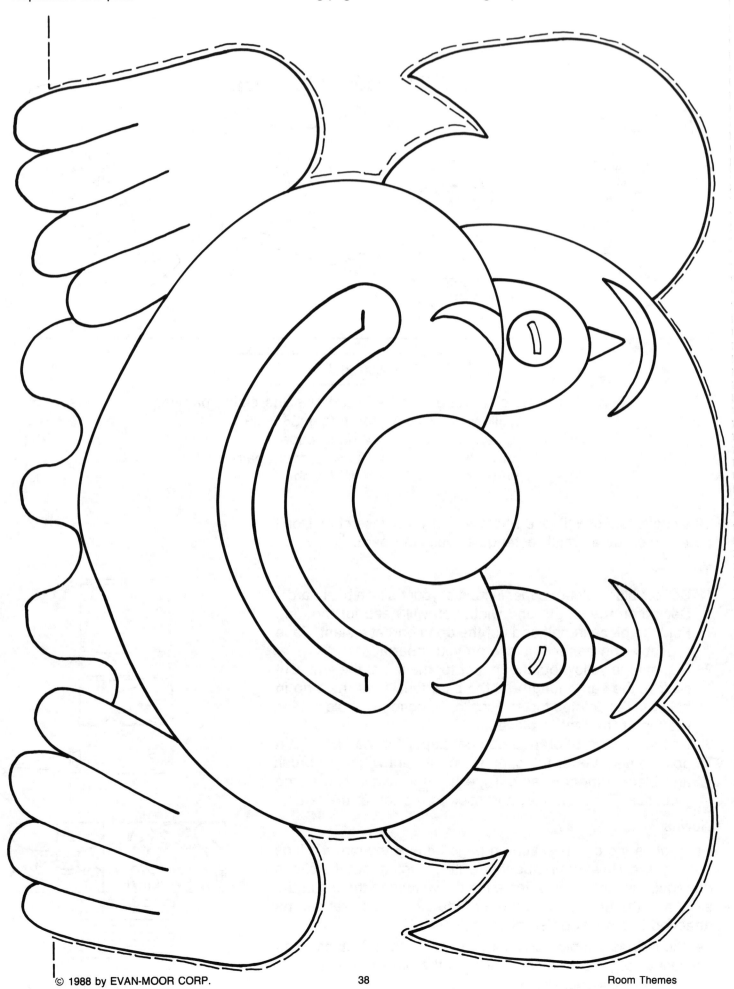

38   Room Themes

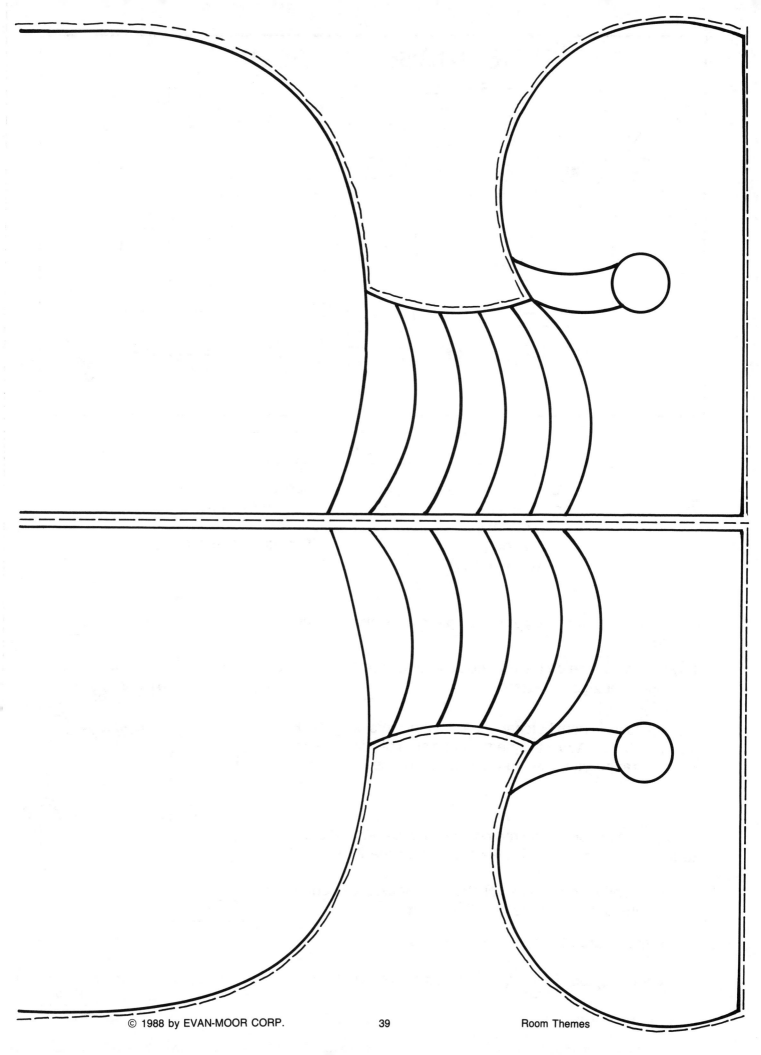

39 Room Themes

Tame these numbers!

Materials

- Reproduce the lion face pattern on page 41
- Butcher paper
    - orange (mane)
    - yellow (body)
- Construction paper
    - red (stands)
    - black
- Tag strips (flashcards)
- Orange yarn

---

1. Reproduce the lion face pattern on page 41. Color it yellow.

2. Lay the lion's face on the orange butcher paper. Cut around the face in a zigzag pattern.

3. Cut a yellow hill from butcher paper for the lion's body. Make the bottom 12". Add a tail made from a strip of yellow paper. Put an orange yarn pompon on the tip of the lion's tail.

4. Fold up the bottom of the red construction paper and staple to form a pocket. This creates a stand for the lion.

5. Cut the caption from black construction paper. Also cut out the numbers and pin them to the stands.

6. Make flash cards to stick in the pockets.

sets of objects   computation cards $6+1$ place value 2 tens / 6 ones

Reproduce this lion face pattern for the Tame these numbers! bulletin board.

Trapeze

READ
about the
Circus

1. Cut the dancing bear's body from brown tag using basic shapes.

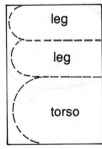

leg	arm
leg	arm
torso	ears head

2. Cut a tunic from red construction paper. Cut the tunic the same size as the bear's torso. Then cut out the neckline and arm holes.

3. Cut slippers from pink construction paper.

4. Cut a hat from red construction paper. Add pink circles and a pink pompon.

5. Cut a nose and eyes from black construction paper. Paste these to the dancing bear's head. Add the rest of the details with black felt pen.

6. Write the caption on the tunic with a felt pen.

7. Pin book jackets in the dancing bear's paws.

Swing into _____

month

Materials

- 1 standard calendar face
- Construction paper
  yellow 8'' X 18''
  white 4'' X 5''
- Blue butcher paper (background)
- 1 paper towel roll
- Yarn
- Felt pens

S	M	T	W	TH	F	S

1. Cut the trapeze flyer from the 8'' X 18'' yellow construction paper. Add details with felt pens. Glue the head and hands to the body.

yellow paper   BODY   2½''   5½''   2½''   7''   white paper   HEAD   5   4''   HANDS

2. Fold up the legs.

4½''

3. Thread the yarn through the paper towel roll to make a trapeze. Slip the acrobat's legs around the roll.

4. Cover the bulletin board with blue butcher paper. Pin everything in place on the bulletin board. Add the caption with a felt marker.

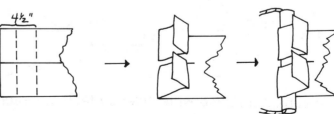

The Elephant Parade

This is a useful bulletin board idea for that long, narrow space above your chalkboard.

Use this elephant parade to reinforce language or math skills you are working on with your class.

Reproduce the elephant pattern on page 45.

- Invite students to write couplets about the circus on the elephants' blankets.

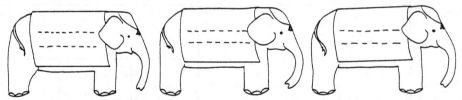

- Practice skip counting by putting one number on each elephant.

- Write facts or vocabulary words about the circus on each elephant's blanket.

- Do an elephant unit and write science facts on each blanket.

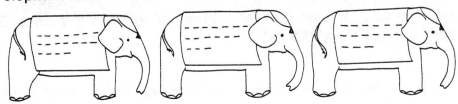

     Room Themes

Room Themes

Circus Train Display Board

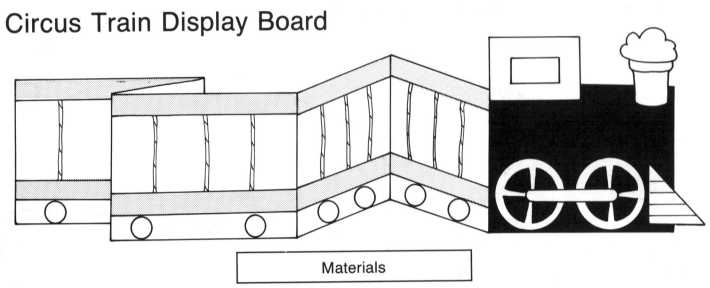

Materials

- Reproduce the engine pattern pieces on page 47.
- 8 1/2" X 11" tag rectangles — 1 per car (in a variety of bright colors)

- Assorted colors of construction paper
- Black yarn
- Cellophane tape
- Magazines

Engine

1. Tape the train cars together with clear cellophane tape. The first rectangle should be black.
2. Cut out the engine pattern pieces and paste in place on the black tag

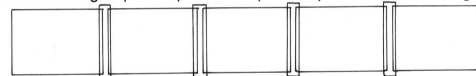

Cars

1. Cut strips in contrasting colors. Lay two on each car. Cut black wheels and paste them below the lower strip.
2. Cut strips of yarn for bars. Tape them down and cover the ends by pasting the two paper strips over them.
3. Cut a 4" x 5" construction paper rectangle for the cab.

Circus Animals Options

Let students cut pictures from magazines and paste them behind the bars.

Have your students create circus animals to ride on the train. The animals might have long necks sticking out over the top of the train.

Paste an envelope on the back of each train car. Then you can slip tag strips or flash cards behind each car.

Uses for the train display board:

- Helpers chart
- Computation drill

- Make it into a train book by attaching children's stories behind each car of the train.

   Room Themes

Engine Pattern

Cut out these pattern pieces, color them, and paste them to the black tagboard.

Step right up and see
the greatest in the world!

Starring in the center ring...

_____
name

_____
date